Before You Become Improbable

Nick DePascal

Before You Become Improbable

Nick DePascal

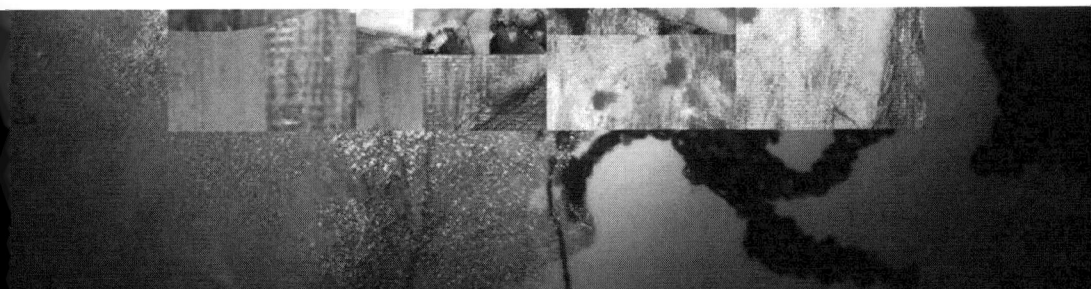

Thanks to the editors of the following journals, where these poems and their earlier versions first appeared: *Adobe Walls, Aesthetix, Breadcrumb Scabs, The Emerson Review, Golden Sparrow Literary Review, The Houston Literary Review, The Los Angeles Review, Monongahela Review, Similar:Peaks:Poetry,* and *Things in Light.*

First printed edition: July, 2014
ISBN: 978-0-9910742-3-5
West End Press/P.O. Box 27334/Albuquerque, NM 87125

Front cover photograph: Lisa Kalberg / *Typography and design*: Lila Sanchez

FOR BOOK INFORMATION, SEE OUR WEBSITE AT WWW.WESTENDPRESS.ORG

I did not deem that Planetary forces annulled—but suffered an exchange of Territory, or World—

I should have liked to see you, before you became improbable. War feels to me an oblique place—

Should there be other Summers, would you perhaps come?

—Emily Dickinson in a letter to T. W. Higginson
February 1863

Acknowledgements

Thank you to John Crawford and everyone at West End Press,
including the judges who selected this book for the
West End Press poetry prize in 2013.

Many thanks also to Lisa Chavez, Dana Levin, Amy Beeder,
Greg Glazner, Dan Mueller, Marissa Clark, Scarlet Higgins,
Bonnie Arning, Nora Hickey, and Natalie Scenters-Zapico for their
various kindnesses and helpful guidance on things poem-related
and otherwise.

Table of Contents

For Erin and Owen
who remind me every day why the world is a place worth writing about.

Family Like a Pack of Wild Dogs
Tucson, 1982

Your mother's floral curtains billow, bunching in the breeze
from an open window. A benediction of sun spills onto green

carpet. *Close the goddamned window, you're letting
all the heat out.* Wise wood buffet, the dark of old blood,

initials etched into the side facing away, for which your father
whooped you so hard. *Nothing, I mean nothing will get out*

that stain. Also the darkened den with the rolling television
and faux wood paneling. The bottles with peeling labels

and illegible names, arranged carefully on the shelf, standing
sentinel over everything. *The first time I tried them, I spent*

the whole night puking in the bathroom. The clothes still laid
out on the bed. There were those two curling iron scars

on your neck, and the yellow linoleum peeling by the sink.
There wasn't anything we could do for her. Wedding whites

and funeral blacks are our family colors. Across the yard,
the gloomy mulberry where our initials are carved in jagged

letters. *It was clear no one could stop her; you could see she
had it coming.* You're sleeping in the garage on a couch

patterned similar to your mother's curtains. She sewed them
herself and had a dress cut from the same design. *And I said,*

Lord, if you help me here, I promise to be a better man.
Your sister laying in a curdled heap; your sister bunched up

like those floral curtains. Your sister like a breeze from the open
window; she's around here somewhere I'm certain. *How many*

times have I told you, how many times have I, how many times.
Leaves turn the color of that waxy linoleum. They abandon trees,

commune and glitter, dragged along the gutter, waiting—
When you wake up, you'll remember nothing.

Autumn in an Old House

My wife is heavy, round.
A brick laid on a bubble.
Thick the smell of smoke

from the open stove. The last
branch peeled of leaves bends
in the wind. Part of the trick

is to keep moving. Part
is to stand totally still.
I measure from her hair to

the tips of her toes six times
a day. It's like a prayer. She
is growing wider, stronger,

her legs and arms stretched
out to make an X in the first
snow. We have borrowed

nearly everything we have
from others. The cat killed
another bird, dragged its body

to the doorstep, chewed on
the wings in the corner. Every
thing can be propitious if we

only want it to be. My wife
buries the body in the garden,
promises great things in spring.

And then I drove until the car ran out of gas

Before you become improbable, consider
the weather, the summer of self-loathing
and Smiths' albums. Driving by the Salton
Sea, naked palms wishing we'd stop

for a picture or a picnic, anything to break
up the horizon's monotony. I'm not there
with the cracked, half-buried boats, the palms,
or anywhere at all, really, but I am twisting

myself into being through a set of rigorous
mental exercises. Smoking pot behind
a grocery store we hover like horses hover
under a tree in the rain. You, licking my

arms like postage stamps, and me setting sail
from the dumpster with my pants around my
knees. But no one can take a joke anymore—
not the checkout girl, the produce manager,

or the janitor with his musical ring of keys.
I'm breaking out of jail, shaving my own
head, wrapping myself in white bandages
like a beautiful nurse, tending to my own needs.

Fat Banker

The world moves on with
or without you

one hand poised with a red pen
the other rubbing at your stained tie

I can imagine you were
an ugly child with a beautiful mother

I can imagine your hell
is smudged ink

and mustard on your white shirt
I can imagine you masturbating

to the miraculous phone sex
advertisements on late night TV

that haven't changed since the 80's
that same blonde woman with loose

curls you remember from your teenage
years hinting at sublime things

you'll never know
how do you sleep with all those

rejected souls flapping around your head
how do you eat with all those bones

in your mouth your head a blood red
melon atop the body of a pig I know

that technically you're not to blame
that behind you stands an edifice

of rules and regulations several miles long
and several hundred feet tall maybe even

state and federal law and yet and yet
here you are right here and I want to sink

my teeth into the thick folds of your neck
and steal back a little of the life you took.

Wife's Monologue on the Occasion of a Seventh Wedding Anniversary

Fleet-footed night arrives
with a fistful of feathers, and I

                am emptied from the neck
                down.

You, on the other hand, come
wearing a suit of armor chinked

                and rusted from your
                last battle—

bringing me stuffed olives soaked
in brine. To live beheaded is

                difficult but possible, trusting
                my lower half to whatever

history crowds the halls of my
castle. How does one keep

                loving as one grows older?
                As the sun burns our skin

to hard brown, and the climb
of our years grows steeper?

                As the nights turn colder,
                and the cracks in our skin grow

deeper? Remove your helmet
your scabbard your mail. Have

                a drink of brandy. Touch my face
                just there. Feel my teeth chatter—

wound tighter than a piano
wired with methamphetamines

                and gun powder—the music,
                the very air around us sprouts

wings and shatters. From
the ruins reconstruct my face

           to resemble the mounted
           boar's head on the wall—

a taxidermist's dream.
And like a well-trained doctor,

           scalpel-handed, poised over
           the body bound for incision,

make your mark on me lasting,
but invisible to all others.

Beatrice's Lament

Wanderers wander, squander that intensity
of light that makes us human. What was Dante's
blunder? Uncovering Hell, or delighting
too much in its tortures? Confusing jealousy
and hunger? I wonder – poets often try too hard
to square the world away, until one day the world
encircles them. Those dedicated ambassadors
of bad news. And then? The end. And after?
Their punishment: watch as fat birds alight
on their shoulders and peck out their eyes.

Awards Committee

Dear artist please step forward and claim your prize.
Pay no attention to the mirrors and strings. Instead,
consider where within our dreams reason lives, and why?
Don't think of those dying islands where the ground splits open.

Pay no attention to the mirrors and strings; instead
try channeling the angels, try angling for a grub or worm.
Don't think of those dying islands where the ground splits open.
Like the fat, black bird nesting in the sockets of the dead,

try channeling the angels, try angling for a grub or worm,
and imagine the earth as an enormous skull rotating
like the fat, black bird nesting in the sockets of the dead.
You sing, *death is everywhere, in every home,*

and imagine the earth as an enormous skull rotating
on a fingertip. Because history is a lot of dirt and graves,
you sing, *death is everywhere, in every home.*
Waiting in the wings is a new flock of suitors balancing

on a fingertip. Because history is a lot of dirt and graves,
we divide your winnings, consult the currency exchange.
Waiting in the wings is a new flock of suitors balancing
their checkbooks on their knees, pens poised, ready.

We divide your winnings, consult the currency exchange.
You flush at the sight of all that green and forget
the checkbooks on their knees, pens poised, ready,
to make an offer for the next spot in our coffers.

You flush at the sight of all that green and forget
your manners, but will you hurry please? We want
to make an offer for the next spot in our coffers.
Squawk on top of rubble, city squares, and think about

your manners. But will you hurry please? We want
what's best for this magnificent glass building, to watch you
squawk on top of rubble, city squares, and think about
the poems we were promised in your letter. A list:

what's best for this magnificent glass building, to watch you
consider where within our dreams reason lives, and why?
The poems we were promised in your letter, a list.
Dear artist please step forward and claim your prize.

Winter in an Old House

My wife is Christmas
lights pinned up high
on a balcony as winter

closes around us. Our
bodies—porous as the walls
of the house—shriek

at the slightest touch.
Threaten to crumple
if we don't comply

with their demands: stoke
the fire; light the pilot;
fill the rooms with heat

and a violent longing.
Nothing is silent. Every
thing creaks or moans,

even the animals outside
hunkering down in brush.
A fever is required. A long,

cold sweat into morning.
Backs of our hands black
with soot, tears, the smoke

when the flue wouldn't open.
There is a tub but no hot water.
Wind is wicked and makes us wander.

Airport Elegy

Christmas: an airport newsstand

        in the Midwest—

glossy ad in a glamour magazine:

        Audrey
        Hepburn

dressed in black,

    frozen in some absurd

        dance—what has happened

          to that type of beauty?

All hair and eyelashes

        black berets,
        red fingernails—

          dreaming of a glass apartment

in New York City—

where are the pregnant

        teens wailing paeans
        and scattering peacock

feathers in her memory?

Where are
    the acolytes
to probe
    her mysteries
like a tongue
    over missing
      teeth?

Why is there no Bible

        for her?

Of sing-song limericks

      and hymns to beauty,

of sad hellos
    & goodbyes?

No oil painting
of her breakfasting

    in mid-air,

floating—
    a first miracle.

There is no substitute
    for the inexact sadness
        of airports, blind mumble

and motorized walkways.

Screens filled with arrivals

      and departures, like credits

rolling on a film about
the Midwest winter.

A few moments of peace
      arrive on tinny wings—
voice over the loudspeaker
      announces:

Remember
never to leave
your baggage
unattended.

Sex in an Old House

My wife is an auctioneer,
selling off my body parts
one by one. She takes a

finger in her mouth, then
a hand, then a whole arm,
biting down fairly hard.

This is the game: to be
the last one standing; to
be the one who got away,

or the one who won't go.
Her nipples are dessert plates,
my hands the carving blade.

I put on her underwear, and
gyrate slowly to the chords
of "Purple Rain." She is

the skillful pilot, the curvy
ghost who can't leave. Flying
us low over the bed clothes

and bowls of old pasta, cups
of cold coffee and the telephone's
suspicious gaze. She stands and

stretches, still and naked as a frieze,
bumps raised on her skin like fires,
coaxing every softness out of me.

Vanity

I crack an egg into a skillet,
          watch the edges firm and brown
          but keep the yolk very nearly raw—

I spend a lot of time considering
          what color tie to wear—

I see other people as cracked
          imperfect mirrors onto which
          I can project my transgressions—

I constantly imagine I'm the sole
          survivor of an horrific air crash—

I remove from my pocket a gold
          watch—

I open my coat and let loose
          an assortment of birds—

Would you like to hear the specials?

No. Today I am only cataloging
          the world's sins—

I am only making notes in my black
          book—

This is just a test
          a drill
          a run-through in the event
          of a real emergency—

I am only preparing for the inevitable—

I am only making plans
          for a great escape—
          for the after party—

I stopped trying years ago—

I am a twenty dollar bill
carefully palmed—
a drunken string quartet
leaping from a balcony—

I am the savvy dead man slickly
pocketing the profits
of the living.

And then I painted myself with a halo

I was talking, and then you were talking,
and we kept being interrupted by clouds
marching across the sky, and a plane
that flew in front of the sun for a moment

and everything went dark. It was history,
that moment, a telltale sign from the deity
in charge of combing hair. And you painted
a portrait of me with a cockatoo, and then

I painted myself as a saint with a halo
and my attendants were angels and I was
telling God about which Bruce Springsteen
record was the best, and about the bad taste

that was still in my mouth from birth. His mother
was hungry too. And she whetted her tongue
on a stone, and sharpened it to a point we can
see from space. And we were talking together

at the same time, our words overlapping and
blending, the talking becoming birds and puffs
of smoke in the roar of jet engines, each of our
sharp tongues stabbing at the air over and over.

Husband's Monologue on the Occasion of a Seventh Wedding Anniversary

My hands transmitting to a beloved in an empty hotel,
a signal strong, profound—a sound out in the hall,
an incoming message, a dim and separate hell.
Of all the things lost we counted ourselves among them.

A signal strong, profound—a sound out in the hall.
A black button sewn with white thread, signifying marriage.
Of all the things lost we counted ourselves among them.
We were allowed to forget that neither of us was primal:

a black button sewn with white thread, signifying marriage.
There was one time, and then another. And after drinks
we were allowed to forget that neither of us was primal.
There are always times when the white thread frays a little.

There was one time, and then another. And after drinks
perhaps we realize that all love is merely accidental, that
there are always times when the white thread frays a little,
slackens or tightens a bit, threatens to come undone.

Perhaps we realize that all love is merely accidental, that
this house no longer holds the old intimacy. The passions
slackening or tightening a bit, threatening to come undone.
And flight, the idea of flight, pressed between the temples tells us

this house no longer holds the old intimacy. The passions
alleging any number of crimes. But over the ritual clatter of glasses
flight, the idea of flight, pressed between the temples tells us
the patterned plates are stacked neatly in their cupboards,

alleging any number of crimes. But over the ritual clatter of glasses,
an incoming message, a dim and separate hell.
The patterned plates are stacked neatly in their cupboards,
my hands transmitting to a beloved in an empty hotel.

While My Son Sleeps in a Cradle Next to Our Bed

Each night is a new
cruelty devolved to
the approximate shape

of a cudgel, another
chance to consider:
what is there to know

of bliss that hasn't
already been etched
on the million stones

of graves? I find myself
longing for the pleasant
drug of sleep, to dream of

nothing but the reds
of roses planted years
before I was born—

bloody blooms opening
like chasms when I was just
a boy. Somewhere, doubtless

there exists a prayer
for the rest of childhood,
a prayer to forget the long

dead and their prophecies.
I remind myself I'm lucky
to be alive, to have survived

the daily crush of angels
on the head of this pin.
And for a moment sleep

comes with the clarity
of a rung bell in autumn,
sprung from the head

of some god and hollowed
out to ferry blood through
our veins——'til an ambulance's

shrill tears a hole in
the night. A vulture
picking the city's corpse

clean, dissolving dreams
blossoming just beneath
my skin. I rise, ill-rested,

and watch the brown
haze of the city come
down in the cold morning,

counting all the things
that might go wrong—
an inheritance from

our parents—to constantly
tally up our wreckage,
remaining exactly where

we are and always have
been—prostrate on our
backs and staring up.

Night in an Old House

My wife is a sliver of light
under the door, the crooning
hum of the heaters coming

on at dusk. I've isolated her
scent and bottled it. Two parts
saffron, one part sunset, a hint

of wood smoke. When she's
away I spray it on all the furniture
and plants and sleep until she

returns. The percolator complains,
anticipating her touch. She draws
maps on my back in yellow pollen,

strangles flies with strands of her
hair. I whistle her favorite song
to call her back, but mangle the tune

in the dark. Snow piles up outside
the front door: knee-high, waist-
high, chest-deep, more. Finally

she returns, stuffs cotton in her
ears, and quotes Rumi in her sleep.
Collecting moonlight in her

cheekbones, she shakes it out all night
onto the sheets and pillows. She is
the house, south-facing, warm.

Winter in Hartford

It was evening all afternoon.
It was snowing
And it was going to snow.

     —Wallace Stevens, *"Thirteen Ways of Looking at a Blackbird"*

Snow falls on houses and cars,
creating lines where none were before.
You were born in cold weather

and reborn yearly in the angles of winter.
Always a ready voyeur
on some eternal February morning,

at a cabin outside of Hartford with windows
nearly frozen over, you just managed to make out
a scene indescribable,

except in poem:

A coven of crones
burning their wigs and nylon stockings
into pools of sticky saliva

and cackling at the sight—
a return to youth—which for you
would hold the secrets of seasons,

the changing of old guard to new.
And here you would remark
that sometimes there was a cabin

and sometimes there wasn't,
but that nature's constant revolutions
reflect only our own interior gloom.

52 Horses

What do you do
with 52 slaughtered horses?

Or with 52 horses
soon to be slaughtered?

Certainly the glue market
is constantly expanding

or at least remaining flat
in terms of demand. But

for 52 horses, thoroughbreds
did I mention, this is hardly

reassuring. Horses are smart,
they understand faces, they can

smell fear and the blood
in your heart. And one wonders

what will happen to all that blood,
roughly 468 gallons of the stuff,

and the meat, what of the meat?
Think of all the mouths that could feed

and eating a horse is not wholly
unheard of, but again, this is outside

the scope of horse consciousness, see,
I'm only wondering exactly how much

the horse knows. From the look
in your eyes, they'll know what's

up—the glistening corners, the averted
gaze— when you usher them

into the trailer, still reeking
with the last horse's excrement,

and you sadly pat them, maybe
give them an apple where before

a carrot would've sufficed. *Say
no more* their black eyes whisper,

I know where this is going.
And they don't care much

for their dead owner, or his farm,
or his city-dwelling son, who said,

*What the fuck I am going to do
with 52 horses, just get rid of them*

like they were stocks to sell. Storms
roll long and slow, and the rain

washes the fields of pasture grass
clean. But the smell, the smell of horses,

whatever that is, remains, like a sticky
handprint, indelibly marking the plains.

Late Winter Sonnet

Her eyes, by now, gone milky white, the hands
rheumatoid, fingers curling like the smoke
she spoke through—acrid, gauzy—all the grand
wisdom gone, the body pitted and broke
and mostly spent. Remembering how, as a girl
the pianos played themselves, and the breath
of each machine was a black flag unfurled—
what reason could she have to think of death?
Sweat memories and all the life in them
prickling the skin in the red sun above
budding leaves. Each spring a new pendulum
that swings in perfect mockery, like love.
"Dig a hole, not so deep," her last request,
"so that I see the sky from where I rest."

Artifacts

This, then in the interest
of time and of raising
our mothers to saints
from martyrs

                a finger bone
                a tuft of hair

we will never

        be rid of them

                truly—

and why should we?

They are the doors
that have opened.
They are the linoleum

we have eaten lunch off of—

                a finger bone
                a tuft of hair

this, then, for posterity
and to be on the right
side of history—always
tearing our mothers to pieces.

Cathedral

How many bones have you uncovered,
brushed off, and rebuilt to a cathedral
of dreams? If I could distill all your
arguments to a single word, it would be
"live," or else "leave." The snow is almost waist
deep, the sky's pieces missing – already
this excavation has gone on longer
than was needed – yet you dig and dig, picks
and shovels upsetting the clay-rich soil,
occasional clang of rock on metal
combines with the muted shake and ruffle
as birds turn and wheel at the sound of ringing
bells in that cathedral you're destroying,
piece by piece, to rebury all the bones.

Day in an Old House

My wife bakes bread for an
evening wedding in the early
morning before the fog has

burned off and the birds begin
their chirping ritual. She twists
her hair into a loose bun, shovels

more coal into the furnace. I rake
my eyes along the bright lines
of her body, burying my nose

in the tanned landscape of her
neck. Outside light filters green
through leaves and the cat paws

at a dead thing. This house is
like a bivouac. The days roll by
like a tank made of wind. Where

isn't the beauty in all this? She
picks out my shirt and tie. I watch
her dress and undress in an oblong

mirror, casting aside the few things
she brought along to wear. It's time
to leave when the light coming in

the window is equal to the light
going out. The wedding is lake
side. I marry her again and again.

The Contract

There is a certain pattern in your work—
the old professor says, blowing smoke
through the open window of his yellowed

third floor office, the room so cold you
could see your breath—*like a Buddhist
monk picking flowers. There is worth*

in failure—his body failed to keep
the spots from growing on his lungs—
like the slow march of an army in retreat.

I spend so much time looking, but not seeing.
*A poem is made with the sharp precision
of an autopsy.* Imagine everything in clean chrome,

the instruments delicate on a tray. *First,
remove the organs, each in turn. Then probe
and weigh them to discover where the failure*

occurred. He tells me, *the only way to pass
through life is drinking in all we can—the soul
is a thirst—always so long between drinks.*

He falls silent, smoke dissolving, absently ashes
his cigarette onto a volume of Blake. And even
then, amid the many dead that populated

the blanker corners of his mind, did he ponder
a final metaphor—body as contract—and whether
his was carried out or broken.

Spring in an Old House

My wife wakes to the smell
of oranges, cooks bacon to
crisp, collects the drippings

in a can to feed our children.
The woods are an open field.
This is the stupid math of loving

another human being. Counting
chickens until the sun shines
through the cracks in the walls.

In winter this place is haunted,
but now: the pantry is stocked,
you can drop a bird from a hundred

yards, and even the trees are giving
milk. We walk daily to the lake
with a thermos of coffee and a book

about birds. I know a lot of words,
my mouth can make the shape
of many sounds, but I am silent

this morning. The lake looks
impenetrable, bright, and blue. We
row a boat out and remove our clothes.

My wife cuts her hair and then mine.
We join hands and stomp our feet
in time. Spring is ritual put to song.

Fragments

endless morning

sky of

      exposed wires

            matins

your forecast today calls for

      extreme unction

make no mistake

a swallow coos
in the barn

            waiting around to die

that song in your heart

              means unimaginable pain

for others yes

alone wake up

demons in your headlights
a sudden influx of locusts
box of wine in bed
the uncertain future of air travel

        a car backfires
        in the cool dark

      a rifle's report

no amount of
sequins
ticker tape
words

        will return

this morning

to you   afterwards

purple bruise

good girls and boys

all know

that nothing goes according to
         God's plan

See for example figure 1 or

         simply replace the "stay fresh" seal

      no one can define for me

the words carved on her

      shoulder blade

    impossible

Yes/No check one or both depending on

    the oracle

a handy home kit
    to suit all your needs

Tattoos as advertising

We're sorry but
    we're currently unable
        to process your request

Synergy

The boss calls a meeting, extracts three teeth
from each of us, asks, *What animal are you*

in the office? I have trouble comprehending
the grunts and hoots of my co-workers.

The smooth ivory of the board room table
gleams like a cat's eye, calls us back time

after time. The tiger picks its teeth with a bone
from my neck. The hyena watches us walk

the halls. The parrots bob their heads back
and forth like colorful metronomes. It's hot

in the office today. I strip down to my stripes
and fur and paw at the neutral carpet. The days

slide by like entrails from a corpse. We divine
our duties and responsibilities from them. We

sniff the storms out and write memos about
the weather. Square the circle. Make synergized

decisions about the chain of command. Who to eat
first. This is the place we're born and raised for,

our mothers chanting phrases from motivational
posters, our fathers crying into their Styrofoam cups.

Syncopation

Of our leaner years
they will simply write

        time passes—

but there's nothing
wrong in the pleasure

        of repetition.

You take the same
route to work each day,

        and I still

hold a fork in my
left hand, though I'm

        right-handed—

a habit you find
simultaneously maddening

        and endearing.

We live close to
the bone, but occasionally

        the meat comes:

I think of driving
home from the hospital,

        our son in the backseat—

*how did we make
this thing?* you ask, but

        I'm too scared

to speak, going slowly,
taking the long way home

        through neighborhoods,

down safer roads. Or
the return to the hospital

        a year later for surgery

and our nervous, secret
laughter at the surgeon's

        bedraggled appearance:

a homeless man in
hospital scrubs masquerading

        as a doctor.

Our son breathes
heavy in his sleep, like you.

        I wake four times

a night just to listen to
paper thin wisps of breath

        make a steady sound.

Bonds

A retired chemist, you expected the world
To maintain its order, to distribute evenly:
To color within the lines.

But that morning you stood in front of the mirror
In a dim, pre-dawn blue, refusing to turn on the light
And reveal an unrecognizable you.

Not the you who had memorized the periodic table,
Who sometimes closed your eyes, drawing boxes
In the air, naming elements and their atomic weights.

Now your face sags, half frozen. Your body under
siege from itself, your body in revolt, calling in
troops and circling wagons. What was it you said

when I left for college? *A spoon never bends itself*
and *Either you make things happen, or let things
happen to you.* So which were you thinking that day

you collapsed—six hours spent clawing linoleum
to reach the phone, and when the dispatcher answered
your tongue refused to move. Do you remember when

life was an equation to be solved? Now heavy
and one-sided, you forget the decimal, drop numbers,
and it all collapses: Stock-still in front of the TV

for days at a time, half of you watches, half turns
away, struggling to draw those floating boxes,
to remember weights and names.

Form

Thank you for your letter, and the stale
coffeecake on the break room table.

And we apologize if we've offended
your baroque sensibilities, distracted

as we were by the businessmen drinking
blood from the skulls of small animals.

We forgot polite introductions and other
niceties of our current society. Rest assured,

the tone of your letter, the angle of the knife
protruding from the cake, did not go unnoticed.

And we've made some changes we think
you'll like. First, consider that all the oxygen

is now recycled. The speckled ceiling tiles
spit and smoke. Notice the sink of raw meat,

the cloven-hoofed secretaries preening
the feathers of their black wings. All of this

per your written request of just last week.
On page 32 of the employee handbook

we've enshrined your motto: "Loss
is a hostile takeover." We appreciate

the lavish sympathy bestowed on us
at the annual retreat and how it reminded

us of childhood and our various past lives.
So, thank you for that, and for the dark

visions you shared with us in the brainstorming
session—running your tongue over your lips,

and clicking your teeth.

Hymn to a Hot City

And why not? Summer, a hundred
and ten degrees, slips by until a smell

drives the neighbors insane. Corpse.
In its bed or easy chair, or slouched

at the kitchen table. Corpse. Knows
its time is up, receives the patrolman

with an easy smile, rolls peacefully
down tenement steps, shrouded,

into the back of a black ambulance—
the one for those who don't need

saving. Everyone dies on a Sunday,
and this is no different. And the apartment?

Business as usual. Where the afterlife
begins in earnest. The flies basking in

the food left gooing, last supper going
green to brown and back. The windows,

foiled over, a gallery to watch a man
struck down, hand to the head, grimace,

nothing else. Or an errant chicken bone
lodged in his throat, disbelief, heaving

himself around the room, fist in his mouth,
a dance, the grand finale, nothing.

Even before breakfast, the dawn takes it
out of you—ask the policeman, or the corpse

on the gurney. Death is a private thing.
This is the way to pass time: loosen your collar,

unwind with a drink, join a choir, and sing
of all the unpleasant ways to die.

And then I woke up under water

Our parents live at the bottom of the ocean.
I was a child when our neighborhood was
submerged in water. Nobody died, nobody
drowned. All the children grew webbed feet

and gills. School was canceled and the building
dismantled. The constant sound was a muted
whir. We threw wood and bricks at the Coast
Guard ships that passed overhead. My mother

drank sherry and kept baking pies. Again and
again the authorities tried to make contact,
tried to rescue us with sonar and deep sea
divers, rope ladders and personal flotation

devices. The sun filtered through and made
the houses glow blue. Eventually they stopped
trying and instead tossed down canned goods.
The boys and girls played baseball and roller

skated in the dark like always. We rubbed
ourselves raw on beautiful algae, swam
between houses and the swing sets in the park.
Promised each other we would never leave.

Loser's Almanac

Your bad luck is just beginning
                                        it said

in a voice honeyed over with layers
of bureaucracy—a bunch of onion

                skins littering the floor.

five thousand blackbirds

                fall from the sky
                exhibiting *internal*
                trauma

another thousand
or so
white doves
                follow—littering St. Peter's
square—

                the point at which the Moon

is furthest from the Earth.

Bureaucrats dressed
in crepe paper leggings

                dancing
                crinkling
                drinking and
                eating:

dark beer and blood
sausage, stalking awkward
through the room like turkey
vultures, the ever present
chins and stench of—
                        the crumpled O
                        of their mouths
        saying no.

Remember when
carrier pigeons
numbered a billion,
all gone now,
all gone—

    best times to plant,
    to bake, to ask
    for money.

Bureaucrats with binoculars—
slack-jawed and diamond-
toothed—up to their fists in
currency, skulls open like atriums,
a candy dish for the beholder,
O the fingers long and reaching
and the nights like paper crackling,

                or think of the honey bee
                colonies collapsing.

    Around
    their necks around
    behind them
    cords and lockets

        bits of hair and
        teeth and
        the ink within
        their eyes
        gone black.

A family is a fistful
        of seeds. *Plant firmly on their backs*
    only after last frost.

Pretend everyone's still alive,
      parading around the backyard
      raking leaves
        and smoking cigars.

Harvest in early fall before
the weather turns, before
the fields burn, before
their gnarled heads
droop to the ground.

    Look for answers, look
    in all the places you can imagine.

On the side of the road an old crow the size
of a dog scuttles among the weeds—black
feathers erect like goose bumps on the skin,
a piece of trash in its beak, the earth inverted
for a moment so that the crow appears to hold
it in its claws—

      birds are dying,
      and we're worried
      since the bird carries
      the soul to the next world.

The proper etiquette
      for mourning the dead
      and the not-dead-yet,

            the alignment of two bodies
            in a given space.

Ask now, still, while you have the chance,
while still you have breath to draw, ask—
what the fuck is going on down here?

Pathology

And there it is, plain as sense can make it:
the limp limbs, pallid skin—*in the absence*
of knowable truth, a fiction is born.
But rather than try to recreate torn
pages from memory, losing patience
stiff fingers pull the tongue, and bit by bit
temples crumble, the world splits reason
and emotion down the middle. After
years of black rain, gardening in the dark,
pulling up roots, eating nothing but bark,
plunging dry hands in pungent soil, laughter
seems a luxury in any season.
The body scarred and creased like an old hand,
unsure of what to do with its demands.

Summer in an Old House

My wife's wet body moves
with a whistle. Every thing
is moist: walls drip, bottles

bleed, and last night a candle
was snuffed by a leak. Even
the ceiling grows mold, shapes

mutating and furred. I wake
to her glowing, and the calls
of birds. The old Singer in

the corner watches and hums
all night, sewing our heads
together with shafts of light.

She snores like a locomotive,
vibrating with the dust of stars.
I get out the microscope to

examine her pores and find
tiny teeth on the hairs of her
arms. Nobody will know us

when we return to the world.
In fact, they've already packed
up our belongings and buried

them in a capsule. The dirt here
so sharp we have to wrap our hands
in hair and diamonds to dig.

Visiting Hours

I visit hospitals
          for a living

like they're going
                out of style

they call to me
          call me at all hours

drunk or sober
                whispering

about their patients
          their parents

          and the speeds at which fluids travel in the blood

all hospitals are pretty
                much the same

I could draw one
in two minutes
on an unfolded
napkin for you

          they know my name

*You look like you
could use a drink*
one will say

I think of them
all the time—

                quadrants
                clean lines
                city blocks
                filled with
                the infirm

I know them
like the contours
of my wife's body—

round belly
heavy breasts
legs long and
calves toned

a map on which
to plot maneuvers
and advances

                    I can call up their scent
                    from memory their singular
                    perfume so familiar that
                    it defies description an intimate
                    smell each of us will know
                                        eventually

I have to hand it
to them

          they are
          everywhere

but the best
hospitals
are hardly anywhere
at all

          like floating cities we pretend
          don't exist until confronted
          with their gray faces

And then I read *Moby Dick* with my eyes closed

And I was the white whale, but it wasn't
about the whale, it was about the ocean—
it was dictated to me by a series of angels,
each one less beautiful than the last. Do you

think Milton thought those floating spots
in his vision were angels before he went blind?
I read by candlelight with the window open
and wax in my ears to drown out the prayers

of acolytes. The moon is not a metaphor for
anything, but we keep pretending that it is,
flogging it past death. In the afterlife the moon
is making metaphors of us, manipulating

our bodies to and fro like oversized garden
chess pieces, lacquered black and shiny,
repeatedly whipping a hose across our knees
until we shout for our mothers. Meanwhile,

the whale beaches itself on Central Avenue
and waits to die, its ribs remade into parking
meters, reading a book about oceans, a splash
of blue on the cover, without ever opening its eyes.

Letter to a Sick Friend

There's no hope for the black boats
circling the whirlpool—

they're too far out and the radios
are broken, speaking in static

with the occasional drift of voices.
Who here, with a show

of hands, has ever found themselves
lost—can't account for hours

or days, tossed on the waves, deposited
on some bleak medicinal isle—

wake here wake, Prospero! That's your cue
to get on stage with your books

and your rags and make something
happen. Confess confess!

Yes! That is the only way to make
the boat row itself, to swim

towards the shore with arms of fire,
pulling and pulling,

leveraging bone against the blank
and salty expanse of ocean

before you. Already the skin around
your lips is tightening, all the names

like white foam slowly disappearing.
Write them in a book

to make it better; to make you remember
the smell of pitch: your way home.

Tonight the black boats will sink;
tomorrow they will sail again.

Entryways

You let me wash
your hair once more
before we shaved
your head—even then,
clumps came out curled
around my fingers,
circled the drain and
disappeared.

—

A bed for you, a story, plastic tubes, a visit, a new memory—
you writhe like the snakes inside you want out, sterile sheets
tinctured with blood, with piss. No one should ever have to ride
in hospital beds while rain and pigeon shit smear the glass
of walkway windows. The lights in their fixtures flicker,
but no one arrives to fix them—we should only live and live
and live, always looking for the next door.

—

A man walks into a hospital—

is this the beginning of a joke
        or something?

A man walks into a hospital,
says, *I'm converting from myth*—

because?

Because it sounds good—

        [myth of magic fingers
        myth of steady hands
        myth of knows-all-
        sees-all-but-can't-be-
        bothered-to-raise-a-single-
        finger]

*because this city's a hellish shithole,
sometimes, white hot garbage light
choking the sky.*

A man walks into a hospital but really
the hospital swallows the man.

—

Warm air, wind and you are new again,
your legs well-muscled, tan, alive again,
pumping the pedals of your bicycle, and yes,
I'm dreaming all of this again, the drugged,
fluorescent lights above your bed working
their black magic on my mind again, the steady
drip drip drip of your IV, and then the rustling
of your sheets.

—

I tell the soul, the spirit, the whatever holds court
in that mystery space in your body: I want entrance,
easy access, a way to read, an ideographic alphabet,
a Braille, a way to see inside. I want permission.
If I think of you as a house, then the question becomes
exactly how to enter. Do I enter through the front
door key in hand, or slip around to the back, wrap
my hand in a towel, and smash the glass of a window?
Or transubstantiate from person to mist and slip in through
the vents? The spirit ignores me, no answers forthcoming.

—

I'm done with the brushed nickel
doorknobs, the brass knuckle

nameplates decorating this place,
denoting historical significance,

while how many are unaccounted
for? Rolling through walkways

in their plastic caskets, smelling
flowers on the shirts of their lovers,

all the knowing whispers, the impenetrable
jargon. A prayer is a glass walkway,

a release, a rare rain on the stinking
streets. Count them—*prayers?*—

as they flutter, fall from fifth floor
windows—a simple reminder

of the slow poison echoing your veins,
hammering your bones, settling as knots

in the pit of your stomach.

—

After four days I finally
go home, visit the neighbor
who watches our dog, shower,
make soup and a sandwich,
when it dawns on me that I'm
walking between two unnamable
things, two things whose meanings
are as vague and ill-formed today
as they've ever been, like a shadow
or a fear, unmoored from anything
the least bit real. And then, I'm on
my knees, disassembling the sink,
tearing out the pipes, fingering
through the grease for just
a single strand of your hair.

Song

All songs are praise,
a buckling of knees
and tender hearts stolen

by gravity. One path
becomes two and the noise
of birds outside the window

disrupts our love making.
You've taken my hands
and built steeples climbing

up to melancholy—a condition
requiring patience and desiring
further questioning. Uncertainly

the brow furrows. Place
cakes and salt before the altar.
Remove clothing and leap

into the water. There is
nothing here for you soldier
that's not available in all

our fine retail shops. Making
and unmaking a bed in early
morning, the country wears

its disease like a red kerchief
in the breast pocket. I am ready
to begin digging again tomorrow.

And then I started living in the movies

Emptying pockets into the crocodile mouth
at the end of the block we cross paths, nod,
and continue on. So much about the world
is totally senseless, we need to feed it quarters

to live. Your waiter has dirty fingernails
and cracks his knuckles incessantly. He's
a method actor masquerading for a part.
The crimson of his jacket is so poetic as to

defy meaning. Okay, this is my stop. Are you
coming up? The night is no creature. More
of a romcom where our heroine forgives
the abortionist and then marries him against

her mother's wishes. Shakespeare was delusional.
A cinematographer without celluloid,
preemptively destroying the world a frame
at a time. I get the feeling the "I" here is feeling

sad. Which is why we can't have nice things.
Because we break them open to see how they
work. Imagine mystery. Believe it exists.
The welcome mat is out and our arms wide open.